PALLET TOWN ON PARADE

3 The page after that (page 21) has a list of other Pokémon that you will have to search through the whole book to find. (These are a little harder!)

4 Two Pokémon mini-stories are taking place from one picture to the next. You can learn about them on page 22.

Can you find the Pokémon?

Look for the 5 Pokémon pictured below!

Pikachu

Clefairy

Squirtle

Charmander

Bulbasaur

LET'S FIND POKÉMON!
1

THE A-MAZE-ING VIRIDIAN FOREST!

Enjoy nature in the Viridian Forest.
Trees and a Snorlax are blocking your way.
Catch the 3 Pokémon below.
Then, can you find your way through
the maze?

Weedle   Slowpoke   Caterpie

ENTRANCE

LOST INSIDE MT. MOON

The caves of Mt. Moon make a really big maze!
Catch the 3 Pokémon below and get out as quickly as you can!!
(Make it all the way through the maze.)

Diglett   Zubat   Jigglypuff

ENTRANCE

EXIT

Cerulean City is Misty's hometown.
A lot of water Pokémon live here.
Can you find the ones below?

Tentacool   Mr. Mime   Poliwag

Celadon City is a big town.
Today is the day of the Celadon Fair!
Go have fun!
All the Pokémon are here for the fair, too.
Have a great time, everybody!

Raichu   Golduck   Porygon

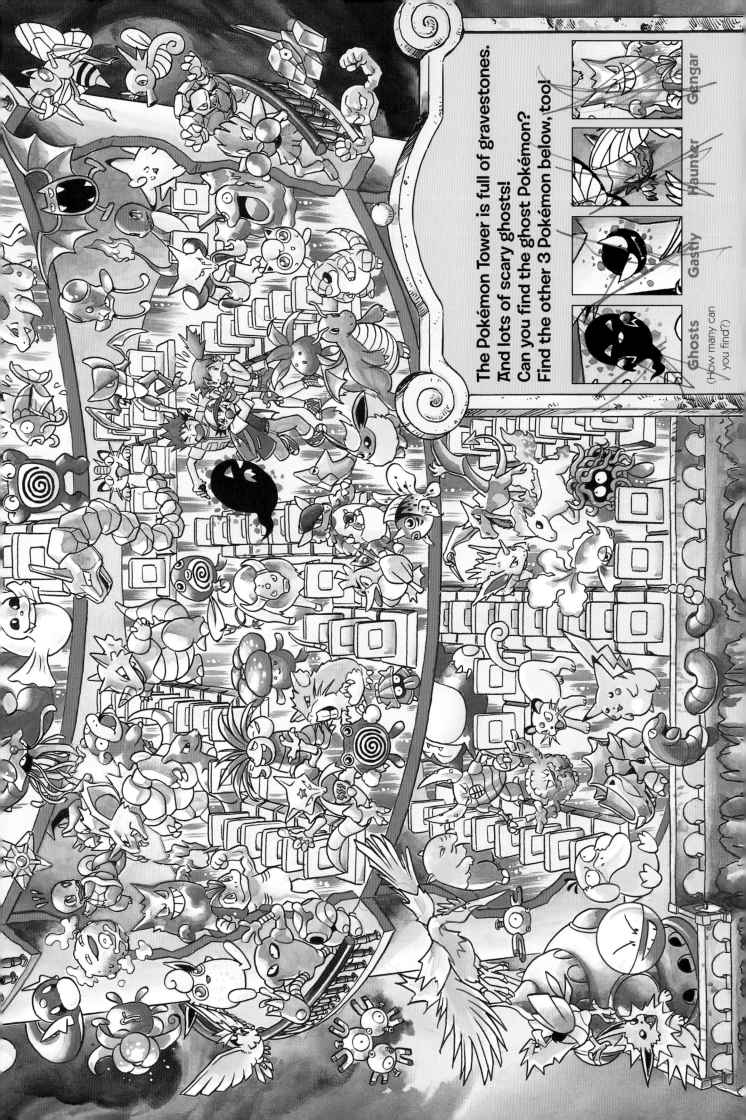

The Pokémon Tower is full of gravestones.
And lots of scary ghosts!
Can you find the ghost Pokémon?
Find the other 3 Pokémon below, too!

Gengar

Haunter

Gastly

Ghosts
(How many can you find?)

You made it all the way to the Safari Zone!
Now you can catch some rare Pokémon!
Try to find the ones below.

Dratini and Pidgey

Mewtwo

Tauros

THE ELITE FOUR OF INDIGO PLATEAU

You finally made it to Indigo Plateau!
Defeat the Elite Four here.
Put yourself in the winner's circle!
And catch the 3 Pokémon below.

Ekans   Venusaur   Slowbro

PALLET TOWN ON PARADE

THE A-MAZE-ING VIRIDIAN FOREST

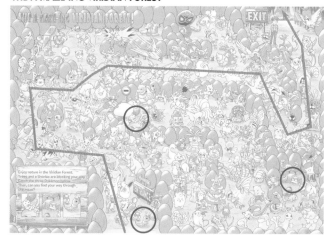

LOST INSIDE MT. MOON

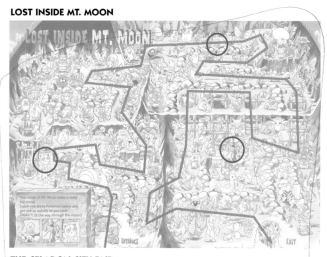

HIDE-AND-SEEK IN CERULEAN CITY

THE CELADON CITY FAIR

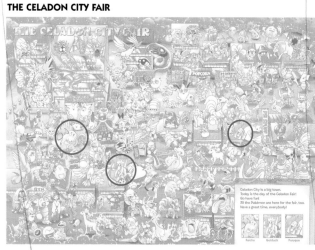

POKÉMON TOWER IN LAVENDER TOWN

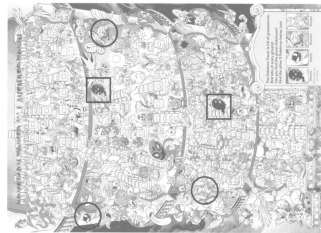

GRAB THEM ALL IN THE SAFARI ZONE

THE ELITE FOUR OF INDIGO PLATEAU

1 There is only one Mew in all the pictures in this book. Where?

2 Can you find the Magikarp on the cutting board?

3 Duplica is pretending she is a Clefable. Can you find her?

4 Where do Doduo and Dodrio crash into each other?

5 Brock is the Gym Leader of Pewter City. How many times did you see him?

7 Where is Machop bowling?

6 The entire Cerulean City picture is shaped like a Pokémon. Which one?

8 Some say not all 150 of the first set of Pokémon are in the first section of this book... What do *you* think?

Answers on page 23!

THE MANKEY AND THE PRIMEAPE
(Where Did All the Bananas Go?)

PALLET TOWN

Mankey is swinging through the woods with its bananas. ♥

VIRIDIAN FOREST

Oh no! You'll get into trouble! You can't just throw your banana peels on the ground, Mankey!

MT. MOON

Now you did it! Primeape went and slipped on your banana peel!

CERULEAN CITY

CELADON CITY

"Munch munch. These are good bananas," says Primeape. Do you feel a little sorry for Mankey?

What did you think you were doing!? Hey! Now Primeape is taking Mankey's bananas away!

LAVENDER TOWN

Ouch!! Look what Primeape did! Machamp has slipped on Primeape's banana peel!

SAFARI ZONE

Machamp: "Grrrrrr."
Primeape: "I'm sorry, Machamp! Here, have the rest of the bananas!"

INDIGO PLATEAU

In the end, Machamp gets one banana for each of its four arms. And Mankey and Primeape cry, "No fair! Boo hoo hoo!"

EXEGGCUTE AND CHANSEY'S ADVENTURE

PALLET TOWN

Chansey discovers Exeggcute! "Huh? Are you my eggs?"

VIRIDIAN FOREST

Chansey: "Hey! Wait up!"
Exeggcute: "A strange Pokémon is attacking us! Run!"

MT. MOON

Oh dear! Oh dear! Exeggcute has been carried off by Pidgeotto!
Pidgeotto: "I caught my dinner!"

CERULEAN CITY

There it is! Chansey's best attack, the Egg Bomb!

CELADON CITY

Direct hit! Good aim, Chansey! (See Chansey strike a victory pose.)

LAVENDER TOWN

Pidgeotto: "Th-that hurt! Did this giant egg just hit me in the head?"

SAFARI ZONE

Pidgeotto: "Ouch! I've got a headache! I didn't really want this Exeggcute anyway! So there!"

INDIGO PLATEAU

Exeggcute: "Thank you, Chansey!" Now Chansey and Exeggcute are friends! ♥

These two stories take place in the pages of this book. Can you find each of the scenes pictured above?

MORE DIFFICULT PUZZLES Answers!

1 Mew is in the upper right of the Safari Zone.

2 Magikarp is in the middle of Pallet Town.

3 Duplica is putting on a show in front of the Celadon Department Store in the upper left of Celadon City.

4 Doduo and Dodrio collided just a little down and to the left of the center of Cerulean City.

5 Brock appeared in five places: Viridian Forest, Celadon City, Lavender Town, the Safari Zone, and the Indigo Plateau.

6 Cerulean City is hiding a Snorlax. (Hold the picture away from you and squint. The hills make up its head and Bill's house is on its left hand.)

7 Machop is bowling in the upper right side of Mt. Moon, a little to the right of the spot where Ash and Pikachu are eating their lunch.

8 It's a secret! You'll have to figure it out for yourself, when you have the time.

● A note to the older folks...

The world of Pokémon is a unique place where a variety of characters have fun and go on adventures. It started as a game for Nintendo's Game Boy® system and grew into an animation series, comic book series, line of toys, stuffed animals, games, and more.

The main character's primary goal isn't to defeat enemies but to see the world, go on adventures, raise the Pokémon he or she has caught, trade Pokémon with friends, and research the Pokémon world using the Pokédex. The world of Pokémon may belong to young people, but you can use this book to play with your children.

Let's Find Pokémon! is designed to teach your children to differentiate shapes and solve puzzles, as well as to aid in their moral development.

LET'S FIND POKÉMON! 2

MON!

GET THE PICTURE!?

ing a great time!

Let's take a picture!

Can you find the 6 Pokémon pictured below?

Beedrill

Weezing

Exeggcute

Clefable

Eevee

Machop

ROUTE 3
TO MT. MOON AND
CERULEAN CITY

POKÉMON MART

Brock is Pewter City's Gym
Leader. He's an excellent
Pokémon breeder and a great
guy to have as a friend. Look
for the 3 Pokémon below!

PEWT

Weedle   Graveler   Geodude

THE PORT TOWN OF VERMILION CITY

S.S. ANNE

VERMILION CITY GYM

Vermilion City Pokémon Fan Club
New Members Wanted

"Why, if it isn't Ash! Remember me? I'm the president of the Pokémon Fan Club."
Are you enough of a Pokémon fan to find the 3 Pokémon below?

Seel   Poliwhirl   Raichu

A detachment of determined Diglett dug this tunnel! And now it's a huge maze! Can you make it all the way through from Pewter City to Vermilion City? On your way, find these 3 Pokémon.

Note: Do not enter tunnels marked with this sign!

Diglett   Raticate   Dugtrio

A SHOCKING TIME AT THE POWER PLANT

They say that beyond the mountains, just before the horizon, lies a fully automated Power Plant.

So use your Surf attack and go! And when you get there, catch the 3 shocking Pokémon below!

Zapdos　　Electabuzz　　Voltorb

The golden skyscrapers of Saffron City glitter in the sunshine, but the city's most precious resource is its Pokémon! Can you find the 3 below?

Lapras   **Hitmonlee**   **Hitmonchan**

Bicycling down the Cycling Road at the seaside is so refreshing... Feel the ocean breeze blow through your hair! Off in the distance, you can see Celadon City. But where, oh where are the 3 Pokémon below?

Arcanine   Vileplume   Magneton

A DAY AT THE FUCHSIA CITY BEACH

The Seafoam Islands lie just above the horizon.
This is where you catch the waves at the beginning of Water Route 19. But it sure is hot! I'll bet some cool watermelon would taste really good right now!

1) How many watermelons can you find?
2) And what about the 3 Water Pokémon below?

Staryu   Starmie   Tentacruel

TO WATER ROUTE 19

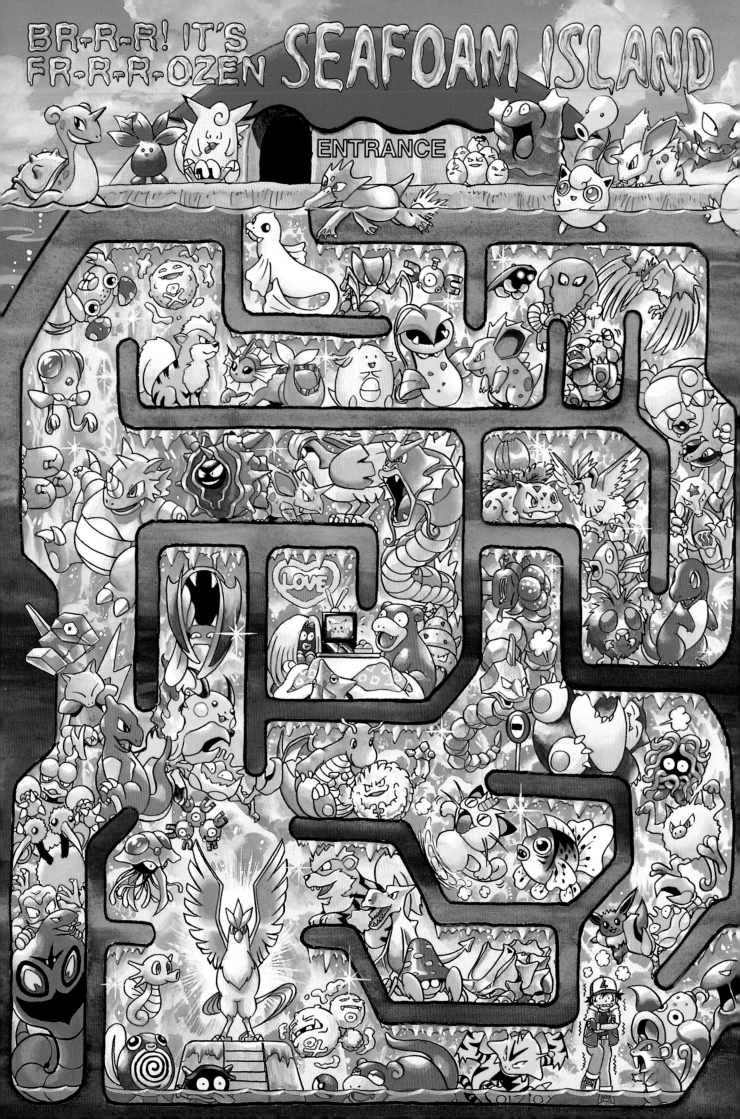

EXIT

Your heart pounds at the entrance to the caves beneath the sea!
But you gather your courage and step in! All that ice could freeze your feet to the floor...
So keep moving, catch Articuno, and find your way through the frozen maze! While you're at it, catch the other 2 Pokémon below.

⊖ Note: Do not enter the tunnels marked with this sign! No cheating!

Articuno   Jynx   Lickitung

CINNABAR ISLAND GYM

POKÉMON MART

POKÉMON CENTER

This island seems to float on the sea. But the truth is, there's a hot volcano underneath! Welcome to Cinnabar Island! Can you catch the 3 prehistoric Pokémon below?

Aerodactyl   Kabuto   Omanyte

BEDTIME IN PALLET TOWN

ASH'S HOUSE

At long last, it's time to go home to Pallet Town... And Mom is so glad you're back! She invites your friends Brock and Misty over for a yummy dinner. Clean your plate! And hope the weather is as nice tomorrow as it was today. Wait! Before you fall asleep, can you find the 3 Pokémon below?

WELCOME TO PALLET TOWN!

Haunter   Nidoran♀   Jigglypuff

PROFESSOR OAK'S
POKÉMON
LABORATORY

Ash and Pikachu have the exact same dream...a dream of Pikachu Forest!

1) Can you find the 6 Pikachu pictured below?

2) Count the Pikachu in the picture. How many are there? Are you sure that's all? (Don't include Ash's sleeping Pikachu on the left or the 6 Pikachu pictured above.)

THE WORLD OF POKÉMON!

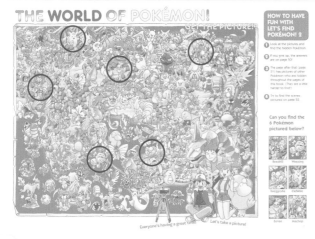

BROCK'S HOMETOWN OF PEWTER CITY

THE PORT TOWN OF VERMILION CITY

DIGLETT'S CAVE

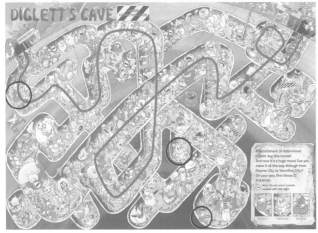

A SHOCKING TIME AT THE POWER PLANT

THE GLEAMING SKYSCRAPERS OF SAFFRON CITY

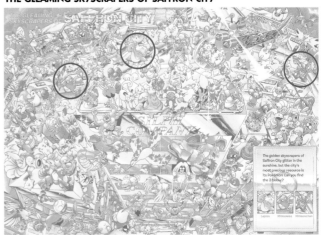

AWAY WE GO DOWN THE CYCLING ROAD!

A DAY AT THE FUCHSIA CITY BEACH

There are 3 watermelons.

MORE DIFFICULT PUZZLES

BR-R-R! IT'S FR-R-R-OZEN SEAFOAM ISLAND

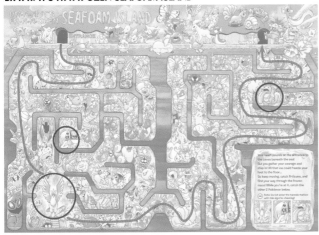

VOLCANO AT SEA CINNABAR ISLAND

BEDTIME IN PALLET TOWN

PIKACHU'S SWEET DREAM OF PIKACHU FOREST

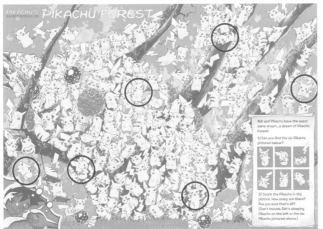

1 In all of the 12 pictures in this book, Mew only appears once! Where?

2 The markings on the underside of this Arbok's hood are different from all the others. What picture is Arbok hiding in?

3 Togepi is so cute! But Togepi only appears once in the whole book. Can you find the little rascal?

4 Where is Charmander digging with this pail and shovel?

5 In which picture is Slowbro gazing hungrily at a bowl of oranges?

6 Did you find the humongous hidden Pikachu picture?

Answers on page 53!

51

CAN YOU FIND THESE SCENES?

Rhydon is taking Growlithe for a walk.

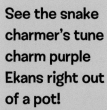

See the snake charmer's tune charm purple Ekans right out of a pot!

Gengar discovers that it's hard to keep your balance with wooden clogs on your feet!

Listen to the lovely Pokémon chorus!

Three heads are better than one, but Exeggutor's unicycle only has one wheel! Fortunately, it looks like things are rolling along pretty smoothly.

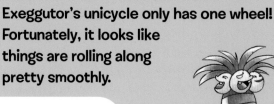

Will that ball ever plop into Machop's cup?

Which Pokémon looks like a tangled ball of yarn?

(The answer is: Tangela!)

Why attach a kite to an Aerodactyl that can fly on its own!?

"Happy Birthday to you!"
"For me!? You're so sweet!"

What would happen if Doduo and Dodrio drank water down all their throats at the same time?

Snorlax finally woke up!

You can find these scenes in the pictures, but there aren't any simple answers to the questions!

MORE DIFFICULT PUZZLES Answers!

1 You can find Mew in Fuchsia City, a little to the left of center.

2 This Arbok displays its unique markings in Vermilion City, to the right and on top of the Vermilion Gym roof.

3 Togepi is teetering on the edge of the lower right corner of the Silph Company building in Saffron City.

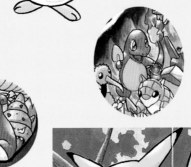

4 In the Diglett Cave, a little to the left of center, Charmander is using the pail and shovel to help Diglett dig.

5 Slowbro is looking longingly at the bowl of oranges in the Seafoam Island Caves, in the middle of the left page.

6 All of the little Pikachu make one great big Pikachu! Hold away from you and squint your eyes a little to see it.

LET'S FIND POKÉMON!
3

TEAM ROCKET'S SE

3 The page after that (page 81) has pictures of other Pokémon who are hidden throughout the pages of this section. (They are a little harder to find!)

4 Try to find the scenes pictured on pages 82–83.

CELADON CITY

TEAM ROCKET'S EVIL LEADER, GIOVANNI

"Jessie, James, and Meowth... your mission is to seek out rare Pokémon, catch them, and bring them to me—*at any cost!!* Start by finding the Pokémon below inside our own secret hideout."

Gyarados

Koffing

Kakuna

Arbok

Nidoking

Victreebel

CRET HIDEOUT

"Oh, dear! What a catastrophe! The Pokémon Center is in complete chaos! Please help me find the 3 missing Pokémon below!"

Seadra   Rattata   Blastoise

"Team Rocket!
Blast off at the speed of light!
Surrender now or prepare to fight!
But first, find these 3 Pokémon—
or else!!"

Wigglytuff   **Primeape**   **Poliwrath**

That's right!

TEAM ROCKET'S GETAWAY!

"Stop right there! Hand over those Poké Balls you stole or face the consequences! And while you're at it—reveal the whereabouts of these 3 Pokémon!"

Dodrio   Metapod   Sandshrew

OFFICER JENNY

Team Rocket is hiding in the forest. All the Pokémon promised to help find them, but now they're too busy playing!

Misty: "Why can't you Pokémon get your act together!?"

Can *you* help her locate these 3 Pokémon?

Pikachu   Starmie   Onix

A DISTURBANCE IN THE THEATER

Everybody loves going to the movies. But today a few trouble-makers have snuck into the theater! Even Raichu is shocked by all the ruckus!

Where are the 3 Pokémon spectators below?

Krabby   Dragonite   Magnemite

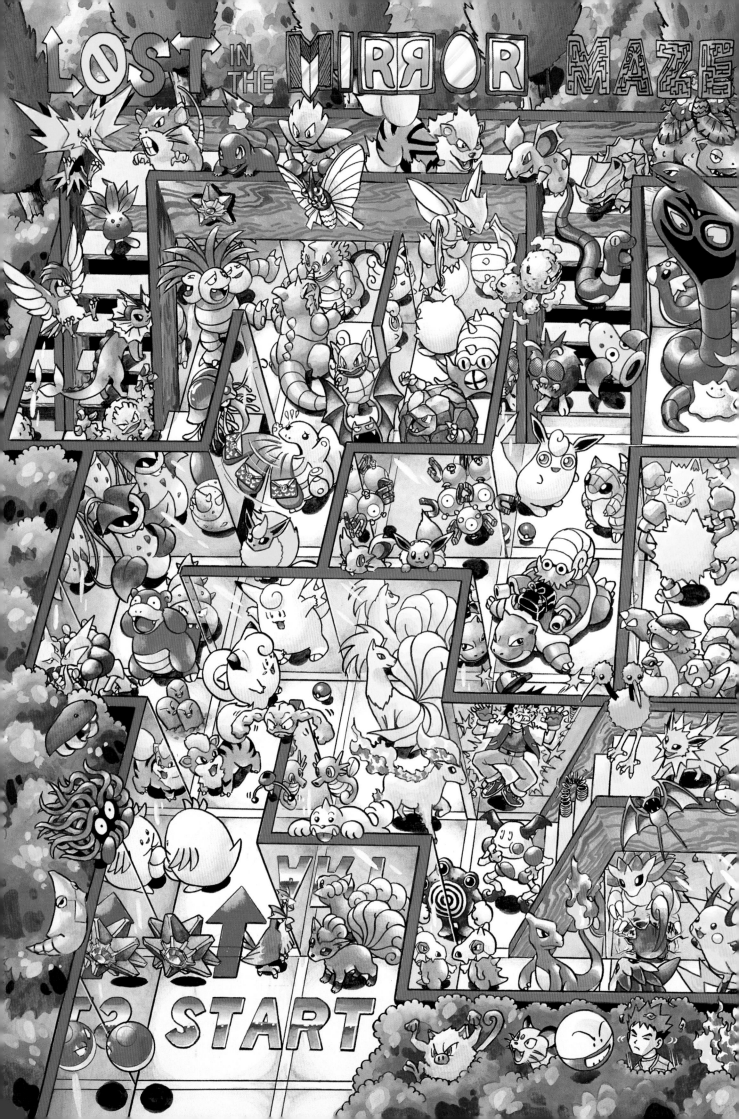

In this funhouse built out of glass and mirrors, you can't tell left from right! Ouch! You just walked into a glass wall!

① How many panes of clear glass are there?(Make sure you're counting glass, not mirrors!)
② Where are the 3 Pokémon below?

Bellsprout   **Ditto**   **Beedrill**

⊖ Weave your way through the maze.
(Note: Do not enter passages marked with this sign!)

SHOWDOWN ON BLASTOISE ISLAND

Jessie: "It's those brats again!"
James: "They're always interfering!"

It's time for a showdown with Team Rocket! But first, find the 6 Pokémon images pictured below.

Squirtle

Wartortle

"Ladies and gentlemen, we're in the midst of a ferocious Pokémon battle! Look! Weezing just used its Smokescreen attack! And Pidgeotto is counterattacking with Gust! What a contest!"

Can you find these, Pokémon fans?

Butterfree   Growlithe   Paras

Pikachu strikes the final blow with its Thunder Shock attack!

Ash: "Pikachu, you were great!"
Pikachu: "Pika, pi chu chu!?"
[Translation: "Yes, but where are these 3 Pokémon!?"]

Poliwag   Rhydon   Nidoqueen

TEAM ROCKET'S TRAINING GYM

Giovanni: "A bunch of kids are preventing you from catching rare Pokémon? You need more training!"

Jessie: "I hate training!"

James: "Training is like work!"

Meowth: "If we wanted to work, we wouldn't have chosen a life of crime!"

Exercise your eyes and find the 3 Pokémon below.

Ivysaur   Charizard   Fearow

WANTED

TEAM ROCKET'S SECRET HIDEOUT
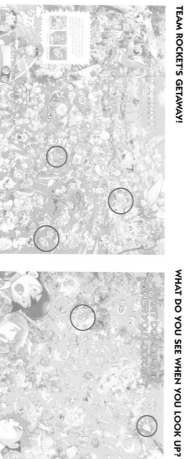

PROFESSOR OAK'S POKÉMON RESEARCH LAB

CHAOS AT THE POKÉMON CENTER
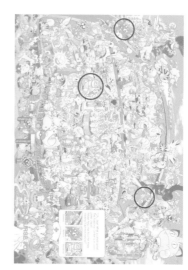

WHERE IN THE WORLD ARE WE NOW?

TEAM ROCKET'S GETAWAY!
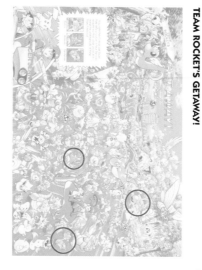

WHAT DO YOU SEE WHEN YOU LOOK UP?

A DISTURBANCE IN THE THEATER
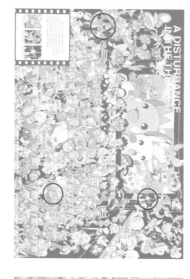

LOST IN THE MIRROR MAZE
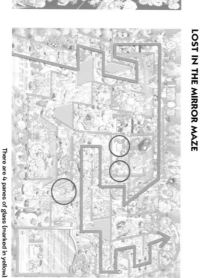

There are 4 panes of glass (marked in yellow).

SHOWDOWN ON BLASTOISE ISLAND
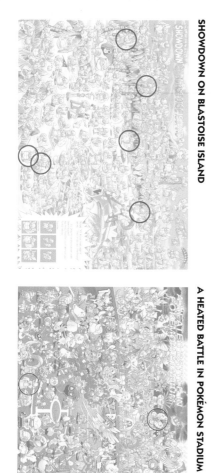

A HEATED BATTLE IN POKÉMON STADIUM
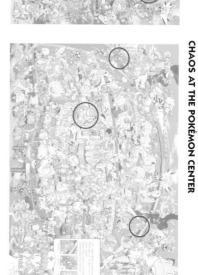

LOOKS LIKE TEAM ROCKET'S BLASTING OFF AGAAAAIN!
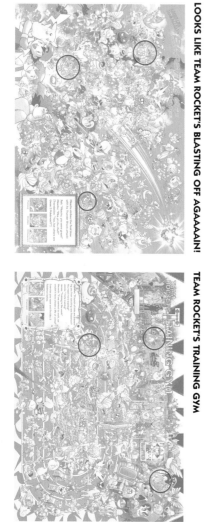

TEAM ROCKET'S TRAINING GYM

80

LET'S FIND MORE POKÉMON!

A "Pid-gey, Pid-gey, Pid-gey!" You've heard of a cuckoo clock, right? Well, this is a Pidgey clock!

B Is Voltorb a cue ball? No, but Voltorb likes to play billiards!

C Mew, the mythical Pokémon, only appears once in this entire book! Where?

D Slowbro and Magmar are playing Pokémon on their Game Boy Color® systems! Where?

E Where is this Pikachu generator located? Don't you wish we all had one to power our video games?

F Whoa, whoa, whoa! Exeggutor is twirling 'round and 'round! Where?

G One of the things you can see when you look up is the outline of a huge Pokémon! Hold the book sideways away from you and squint a little to see it.

H I'm pretty! Oh, so pretty! Where is Jynx admiring its reflection?

I Somebody stop meeeee! Charizard is falling! What will it land on?

J Is this Starmie's "Double Team" attack? Nope! Find the spot where Starmie is rolling, rolling, rolling...

K Go, Ash, go! Where are Richie and Sparky rooting for Ash?

L And the winner is... Can you find the Squirtle sumo wrestlers?

M Oh, no! Now Jigglypuff is hopping mad! Can you find the angry Jigglypuff somewhere in this book?

Answers on page 83!

81

These three stories take place in the pages of this section!
Can you find each of the scenes pictured below?

Story Puzzle #1 — OMANYTE, OMASTAR, AND THE RICE STARS

 **1** Omanyte goes on a hike and takes some rice stars along for lunch.

 **2** Oh, no! The rice stars fell out of Omanyte's grasp!

 **3** And then they plopped right into a lake!

 **4** Suddenly, Jynx appears and offers Omanyte a choice: a silver star or a gold star?

 5 But Omanyte just wants its lunch back.

Poor Omanyte! Jynx already ate up all the rice!

 **6** As an apology, Jynx treats Omanyte to a show, starring Goldeen and Seaking.

 **7** Then Blastoise gives Omanyte a ride!

8 What's in the box? Could it be a new lunch for Omanyte?

 **9** Nope! It's Electrode!

 **10** KA-BOOOM!

11 Guess what!? In all the confusion, Omanyte evolved into Omastar! Congratulations!

Story Puzzle #2 — JIGGLYPUFF'S LETTER

1 Jigglypuff writes a letter! "Hello. How are you? I am fine."

2 Jigglypuff asks Pidgey to deliver the letter to Clefairy.

3 Pidgey flies as swiftly as the wind!

4 Look out! Too late! Pidgey collides with Charizard!

 **5** Kangaskhan finds the dropped letter. Huh? What could this be?

 **6** Kangaskhan tries to return the letter to Pidgey, but Pidgey is nowhere to be seen.

 **7** Lickitung snatches the tasty-looking letter from Kangaskhan!

 8 Hey! Hey! The letter is stuck to Lickitung's tongue!

 **9** Rhydon bumps into Lickitung, and the letter flies up and into Clefairy's hands!

 **10** Clefairy realizes the letter is from Jigglypuff. Clefairy loves getting mail!

 **11** Clefairy answers Jigglypuff's letter by sending an e-mail over the Internet. "Hello. How are you? I am fine."

82

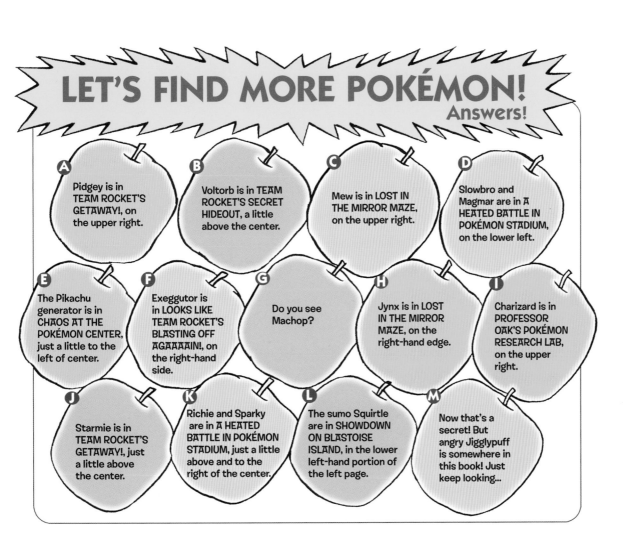

Art by KAZUNORI AIHARA

Original Design/Tariji SASAKI

Special Complete Edition:
Design/Jodie Shikuma
Editor/Elizabeth Kawasaki

Special Complete Edition – 1st Edition:
Design/Hidemi Sahara
Touch-Up/Walden Wong

First Edition:
Translation/William Flanagan
Design/Yuki Ameda, Izumi Evers
Special Touch-Up and Lettering/Wayne Truman, Cynthia Bergst
Editor/Annette Roman

Printed in Malaysia

Published by VIZ Media, LLC
P.O. Box 77010
San Francisco, CA 94107

10 9 8 7 6 5 4 3 2
First printing, July 2017
Second printing, April 2019

viz.com